NATIONAL
GEOGRAPHIC

Spring, Summer, Fall, Winter

David Tunkin

It is spring.

The spring months are
March, April, and May.

It is summer.

The summer months are
June, July, and August.

It is Fall.

The fall months are September, October, and November.

It is winter.

The winter months are December, January, and February.

Look at the calendar.
It shows the spring, summer, fall, and winter months.

January

February

March

April

May

June

July

August

September

October

November

December

Which picture shows spring? Summer? Fall? Winter?